Full Throttle

Land Rover

Tracy Maurer

Rourke
Publishing LLC
Vero Beach, Florida 32964

www.rourkepublishing.com

We recognize that some words, model names and designations, for example, mentioned herein are the property of the trademark holder. We use them for identification purposes only. This is not an official publication.

PHOTO CREDITS: All images courtesy of Ford Motor Company

AUTHOR CREDITS:
The author gratefully acknowledges project assistance provided by Kit Bolton at Downtown Jaguar/Lotus in Minneapolis.

Also, the author extends appreciation to Sean Wagner, Mike Maurer, Lois M. Nelson, Margaret and Thomas, and the team at Rourke.

Editor: Robert Stengard-Olliges
Cover Design: Todd Field
Page Design: Nicola Stratford

Library of Congress Cataloging-in-Publication Data

Maurer, Tracy, 1965-
  Land rover / Tracy Nelson Maurer.
    p. cm. -- (Full throttle)
  Includes index.
  ISBN 1-60044-225-0 (hardcover)
  ISBN 978-1-60044-365-7 (paperback)
  1. Land-Rover truck--Juvenile literature. I. Title. II. Series: Maurer, Tracy, 1965-. Full throttle.

   TL230.5.L36M38 2006
   629.222'2--dc22

                       2006017498

Printed in the USA

CG/CG

Rourke Publishing

www.rourkepublishing.com – sales@rourkepublishing.com
Post Office Box 3328, Vero Beach, FL 32964

Table of Contents

Way, Way Back Then

The Rover history started on two wheels in England. In 1885, the Rover Safety Bicycle used a radical diamond-shaped frame set low with a rear-wheel-drive pedal system to save riders from face-plants. Sales exploded! In the early 1900s, the successful Rover Company expanded into newfangled motorbikes and fine automobiles. World War II forced the company to shift to airplanes, tanks, and tough little farm vehicles.

marque
  the logo for an automobile manufacturer or its models

The Rover Company continued to build cars until money problems forced the firm to close in 2005. With help from investors, the famous British **marque** *may yet rise again.*

During World War II, the Rover Company traded its top-secret jet engine plans to Rolls-Royce for that company's work on heavy-duty tanks.

After World War II, people in England could not afford fancy Rover cars. Overseas buyers wanted trucks and farm vehicles. Rover scrambled to find customers.

The Legend's Start

Maurice Wilks, an engineer at the Rover Company, often puttered around his large estate in an American Jeep from World War II. In 1947, he used a few parts from a Jeep and a lot of parts from a Rover car to create a new **4x4** off-road farm vehicle. He thought an affordable, go-anywhere workhorse might just save the Rover Company until people started buying cars again. No one thought it would become a British motoring legend.

*The Rover Company approved making Land Rovers before Maurice even built the first **prototype**. Amazingly, the new Land Rovers rolled off the assembly line less than a year later.*

4x4
a vehicle that moves by a system that can send power to all four wheels

prototype
for carmakers, the first working model of a design

Workers shaped the Land Rover body from flat aluminum—leftovers from making wartime aircraft. Aluminium, as it is called outside the USA, resists rust. It appealed to the practical British market.

The first Land Rover prototype used center steering. Rover soon switched to right-side steering, like other cars in England.

The 4x4 Land Rovers quickly gained fame for ably scrambling over rocky hillsides, wading through muck and water, and taming other wild terrain. The simple machine was easy to fix, too.

In 1949, the British Ministry of Defense ordered nearly 2,000 Land Rovers. King George VI order one for himself. About 8,000 Land Rovers sold the first year. Suddenly, Rover Company had a winner.

The small engine wasn't fussy about fuel quality—a helpful feature in poor post-War Europe and developing nations. Some ads claimed the Land Rover could even use banana oil.

Land Rover production models changed all the time. Model year updates and tweaks in-between make it difficult today to know a vintage vehicle's year just by its looks. However, the general box shape stayed the same. Even now, Land Rover vehicles share "family" designs.

Today's Land Rovers still use full-time four-wheel drive like the first models.

MAJOR MODEL MILESTONES

1948	Series I Land Rover
1958	Series II Land Rover
1970	Classic Range Rover
1971	Series III Land Rover
1981	Discovery
1990	Defender
1997	Freelander
2006	LR3 & Land Rover Sport

Shhhhh!

Carmakers keep their new projects secret—especially from competitors. Range Rover's first code name was Velar. In Italian and Spanish, velar means to hide something behind a veil. It also uses letters from "Land Rover." Other Land Rover code names:

- *Pegasus* Updates to Ranger for 1994
- *CB40* New Freelander for 1997
- *Tempest* Updates to Discovery for 1998

9

Raves for Rovers

Today, Land Rover builds Range Rover, Range Rover Sport, Discovery/LR3, and Defender. It will also build the Freelander for awhile longer. Assembly work happens in England. Nearly 8,000 people work at the original Solihull plant. This production and testing facility sprawls across more than 300 acres (1214 hectares)—complete with its own lake.

*The full-size Range Rover uses full-time four-wheel-drive. Its **chassis** strength and nimble suspension tackle real off-road adventures in any climate.*

Today's full-size Range Rover blends function and luxury, especially inside. Land Rovers weren't always that way. Designers of early models wanted drivers to feel the road…or the lack of one. They figured uncomfortable drivers would realize when the terrain was too much for the vehicle.

chassis
> the frame that supports the body of a vehicle

horsepower
> a measure of mechanical power; one horsepower equals 550 pounds (885 kg) lifted at one foot (30.5 cm) per second

Fast Fact

Land Rover engines meet strict standards for waterproofing, extra dust protection, and operation at extreme angles.

Fast Fact

A V-8 means the engine has eight cylinders to burn fuel arranged in a V.

*In 2006, Range Rover gained power and torque with a V-8 motor adapted from Jaguar. The supercharged engine delivers 400 **horsepower** (hp) and the standard motor hits 305 hp.*

A Speedy Land Rover (Really!)

People have loved Land Rovers for many reasons, but never for speed—until now. The 4x4 Range Rover Sport features a 390 hp supercharged V-8. Electronic controls limit the speed to 140 miles (225 km) per hour—still plenty fast. Land Rover's advanced engineering allows it to switch into a ready off-roader, too.

Land Rover sold 30,356 Range Rover Sports worldwide in just the first six months of production.

Range Rover Sport is the most **aerodynamic** Land Rover yet. But, the spoiler is just for looks. This is still an SUV (sport utility vehicle) after all, not a sports car.

aerodynamic
air flows easily over the body for greater speed

wheel articulation
the movement or travel of the wheels on the axle so that the tires stay in contact with uneven terrain

*Range Rover Sport offers a new suspension feature for highway handling, especially cornering. For unpaved terrain, drivers turn it off to gain better **wheel articulation**.*

Updated in 2005, the LR3 continued the Range Rover idea of a dressed-up, mechanically sound 4x4. It's just a tad more compact than Range Rover (but it still fits seven people). It comes with either a V-6 or a V-8 engine and all the Land Rover suspension marvels for true off-roading adventures. Called the Discovery 3 in England, it has won nearly 100 major automobile awards.

Fast Fact

In 2005, LR3/Discovery 3 sales topped at more than 53,550 for the year.

The English Discovery 3 and the American LR3 look like twins. Of course, the LR3 has a left-side steering wheel. Less noticeable parts on the LR3, such as bumpers and air bags, meet all of the U.S. standards for pollution control and safety.

The word on the street is that the compact Freelander is out. The good news? Five new Land Rover models could be on the way in the next few years.

Between 1975 and 1986, no Land Rovers were legally sold in North America. The engines could not meet the pollution standards. Now Land Rover builds its vehicles to the toughest California laws. More than 160 retailers sell Land Rover vehicles today in the U.S.

Fast Fact

Since 2000, Ford Motor Company has owned Land Rover. Worldwide Land Rover sales in 2005 hit a new record of 185,120 vehicles.

Jumping the Pond

Land Rover imports to America have lagged behind their debuts in Great Britain. Now they jump the pond (the Atlantic) nearly right away because the engineers design the models for the U.S. market from the start.

Model	Arrived in USA	Lag Time After British Release
Range Rover	1987	17 years
Discovery	1993	8 years
Freelander	2000	3 years

Loyalty and Royalty

Over the years, Land Rover gained loyal fans from across the globe. Once customers try a Land Rover, they're very likely to return to buy the same vehicle model in a newer year. Land Rover owners have also formed clubs to share their love of off-road driving, to swap Land Rover stories, and to trade **restoration** tips.

Land Rover has had some very famous—and loyal—customers. Great Britain's royal family has kept a Land Rover in their stable of vehicles at the Royal Mews at Buckingham Palace since the late 1940s.

Land Rover's Special Projects Department prepares vehicles for the royal family and other important people. For her 1952 **coronation** tour, Queen Elizabeth received a Land Rover painted in her favorite deep red color. She still drives her own Land Rover today.

The Royals weren't the only British leaders keen on Land Rovers. Great Britain's Prime Minister Sir Winston Churchill drove a 1954 Series I Land Rover around his estate.

The loyal royals have issued Royal Warrants to Land Rover, which are the highest British honors a company can receive for providing valued services or products to the Highnesses. Currently, only Queen Elizabeth and Prince Phillip, and their son, Prince Charles, can issue Royal Warrants.

Fast Fact

Land Rover holds four Royal Warrants, including one from the late Queen Mother. Only six of about 800 other Royal Warrant holders have as many.

New Land Rover fans often decide they'd like to own a collector model. Many old Land Rovers run surprisingly well. But die-hard Land Rover drivers rarely give up their old rides. Restoration has become a popular—but not easy—solution. It takes serious time, money, and dedication. Impressive results have helped fuel even more interest in Land Rovers from car clubs and museums worldwide.

Fast Fact

Restorers may spend countless hours simply tracking down official records for the earlier vehicles.

Older Models

In the early years, Land Rover frequently made small changes between "official" model updates. They used up old parts before they started installing new parts, too. Owner modifications also make it confusing to identify older models.

Research & the Internet

The Internet sped up Land Rover research. Because the early vehicles went all over the world, online sites let owners work together to register, check, and document their treasures.

Pre-Production Models

Land Rover didn't scrap its pre-production models like most carmakers. The company even sold some of them.

Most Land Rover collectors prize those pre-production models above the rest.

Heritage Motor Centre

The British Motor Industry Heritage Trust opened the Heritage Motor Centre in the early 1990s to house more than 250 vehicles, including the early Land Rover. The facility also maintains a large document archive. Today many other museums also display Land Rovers.

For Work and Play

Land Rover has always built its vehicles for traveling in rugged locations. The early models offered little "cush for the tush." The 1970 Range Rover combined quality comforts with extreme off-road performance and set the pace for all SUVs that followed (or tried to follow). Over the years, Land Rover vehicles have been modified for all sorts of jobs—from firefighting to rock climbing.

Power Takeoff Units

Early Land Rovers featured power takeoff units just like tractors. These devices could power a harvester, plow, saw, pump, or other equipment.

Fast Fact

Land Rovers have traveled on expeditions to all seven continents.

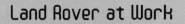

Land Rover at Work

Developing countries or places lacking good roads, quality fuel, or working machinery snapped up more than half of the Land Rovers through 1953. Today, Land Rovers still work hard in remote fields, forests, deserts, and mountains.

Snowy Mountains Project

Land Rovers helped bring water and power to dry regions of Australia. In 1949, the Snowy Mountains Hydro-Electric Scheme imported hundreds of hardy Land Rovers. Workers used the vehicles to help build the tunnels and dams that form this modern engineering marvel.

FC Models

In 1962, Land Rover offered forward-control (FC) models. The cab sat forward, over the front wheels. Many of these sturdy, big rigs became ambulances or "hose cars" for firemen.

Because of the Snowy Mountains project, Australia is home to loads of antique Land Rovers.

The British military has trusted Land Rovers for more than fifty years. Today, many soldiers in Great Britain drive the Land Rover Wolf—a beefed up Defender without the cushy extras. Other nations, such as Switzerland, Australia, and the United States, have also put Land Rovers to work in their militaries. Because Land Rover vehicles handle harsh climates and nasty terrain so well, they've taken on some important tasks over the years.

Land Rover Series II 4x4s sent on desert military duty sported a pinkish **camouflage**. Soldiers nicknamed them "Pink Panthers" or "Pinkies." Later, they called the shortened version "Dinkies."

Land Rover at Work

- Ambulance / medical response
- Farming
- Filming: support vehicle/ on-camera
- Firefighting
- Military missions
- Mountain rescue
- Nature and wildlife photography
- News reporting
- Police, traffic, park, and refuge patrol
- Safari and hunting trips
- School bus
- Scientific exploration
- Tourist transportation
- United Nations security patrol

camouflage
to hide by tricking the viewer, often by blending into the background

Popemobile

The late Pope John II selected Land Rover to build a special armored vehicle for his tours. An assassination attempt in 1982 convinced him to order a bullet-proof design. The Land Rover "popemobile" safely let crowds see him.

In the Movies

Land Rovers have starred in movies. The Series I Land Rover in the 1980 comedy movie, *The Gods Must Be Crazy,* revealed the machine's few short-comings. It also reminded viewers how far Land Rovers could go—the Kalahari desert included.

Land Rovers work hard—and play hard. Off-road adventures appeal to many Land Rover owners, no matter how old or how fancy their rigs might be. Sometimes they use their Land Rovers to reach remote places where they enjoy other activities, such as camping, hunting, fishing, or rock climbing. Other times, driving the Land Rover is the main activity.

Tow Power

Land Rover adds an extra bar across the rear of the chassis for more towing strength. In High Range, a Range Rover can tow up to about 6,500 pounds (2,950 kg). Its powerful but pokey Low Range can tow up to 7,700 pounds (3,500 kg).

Land Rover clubs and dealerships host off-road rallies. Drivers conquer rutted muddy trails, sand dunes, steep ravines, boulders, crevices, creeks and ponds, and other fun **obstacles**.

obstacles
> things that stand in the way or block a path

Suspension

All Land Rover models have superior suspension systems for a nice highway ride as well as ample wheel articulation for off-roading. Depending on the model, the suspension can handle 8 to 11 inches (20 to 28 cm) of up-and-down wheel movement on rough terrain.

treadlightly!®
LEAVING A GOOD IMPRESSION

Land Rover North America supports the U.S. Forest Service's *Tread Lightly!* Program, which works to protect public and private lands.

T - Travel only on trails

R - Respect animals, plants and people

E - Every time you go outdoors, think safety, bring a friend, and be prepared

A - Always leave the outdoors better than you found it

D - Discover how fun the outdoors can be when you Tread Lightly!

Source: www.treadlightly.org used with permission.

"Kitting out" means adding parts, such as brush bars or winches, especially for extreme off-road adventures.

The Muddy Oval Society

Movie stars, rock stars, and other well-to-do drivers might buy Land Rovers for the **prestige**. These people like how they look driving a top-quality SUV. They like knowing they *could* drive it off-road (but they never would). Too bad for them! The green marque really looks best with a dandy coat of mud. The "Muddy Oval Society" is the unofficial name for that group of Land Rover drivers who appreciate off-road excitement.

prestige
reputation for success, wealth, or other positive characteristics

Land Rovers provided specially kitted vehicles for the grueling Camel Trophy competition from 1981 until 1998. This annual 4x4 driving championship featured extreme off-road cross-country challenges.

In 1998, Land Rover sent Freelanders to the Camel Trophy from Chile to Argentina. The compact SUV proved it could run with the big rigs.

After the Camel Trophy events, Land Rover created its own 4x4 mega-competition called the Land Rover G4 Challenge. The first four-week event was planned for 2006 with 18 countries sending competitors to face strategy, stamina, and skill tests.

Land Rover Testing in Extreme Climates

Climate Test	Location	Conditions
Deep freeze	Alaska	-22°F (-30°C)
Scorching heat	Arizona	125°F (52°C)
Drenching humidity	Middle East or Central American jungles	100% humidity

The intense Land Rover G4 Challenge in 2006 required navigating the jungles and cities in Thailand, Laos, Brazil, and Bolivia.

Obstacle courses at Land Rover dealerships show new owners how the vehicles master sharp corners, steep inclines, and other challenging off-road terrain. It also allows the dealership to offer some instruction. Drivers need to adjust to Land Rover's tall and boxy SUV design. They also need to learn what all the dials, buttons, and gizmos do.

Safe off-road driving requires special skills. Which angle is best for climbing? What's the best way to leverage a winch? Making the wrong moves in challenging terrain can wreck any vehicle—even a Land Rover.

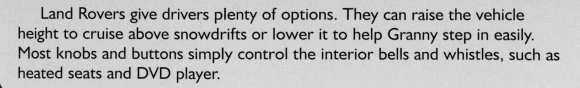

Land Rovers give drivers plenty of options. They can raise the vehicle height to cruise above snowdrifts or lower it to help Granny step in easily. Most knobs and buttons simply control the interior bells and whistles, such as heated seats and DVD player.

In the United Kingdom, Land Rover operates several driver instruction facilities. "Land Rover Experience Centres" offer customers and the public a place to learn and practice off-road techniques. Many driving schools in the USA also provide instruction for off-road challenges.

Many people dream of joining the Muddy Oval Society. A few do it. Their stories and adventures continue to add to the rich legacy of Land Rover.

Glossary

4x4 (FOR bih for) – a vehicle that moves by a system that can send power to all four wheels

aerodynamic (ahr oh dih NAM ik) – air flows easily over the body for greater speed

camouflage (KAM ah flazh) – to hide by tricking the viewer, often by blending into the background

chassis (CHASS ee) – the frame that supports the body of a vehicle

coronation (kor ah NAY shun) – the ceremony of crowning a king or queen

horsepower (HORS pow ur) – a measure of mechanical power; one horsepower equals 550 pounds (885 kg) lifted at one foot (30.5 cm) per second

marque (MARK) – the logo for an automobile manufacturer or its models

obstacles (OB stah kullz) – things that stand in the way or block a path

prestige (pre STEEJ) – reputation for success, wealth, or other positive characteristics

prototype (PROH tah tihp) – for carmakers, the first working model of a design

restoration (reh STOR ah shun) – to return something to its former condition

wheel articulation (WEEL ahr tik yeh LAY shun) – the movement or travel of the wheels on the axle so that the tires stay in contact with uneven terrain

Further Reading

Graham, Ian. *Off-Road Vehicles.* Heinemann Library, 2003.

Hodder, Martin. *Land Rovers: Simply the Best.* Haynes North America, reprint, 2005.

Maurer, Tracy Nelson. *Desert Racers* Rourke Publishing, 2004.

Websites

www.landrover.com

www.fourfold.org

www.landroverusa.com

www.landrover-register1948-53.org.uk

www.royalwarrant.org

www.treadlightly.org

Index

About The Author

Tracy Nelson Maurer writes nonfiction and fiction books for children, including more than 50 titles for Rourke Publishing LLC. Tracy lives with her husband Mike and two children near Minneapolis, Minnesota.